Acedia

Acedia

A Collection of Poems

by

D. Eric Hanson

Acedia
A Collection of Poems

Copyright © 2013 by D. Eric Hanson

Published by:

Hero's Journey Press,
Great Falls, MT
HerosJourneyPress.com
herosjourneyprs@gmail.com

Cover Photo: Mill Creek Road near Livingston, MT
by D. Eric Hanson

All rights reserved. No portion of this book may be reproduced in any form without expressed written permission, except for educational or review purposes and with appropriate credit to the author.

Library of Congress Control Number: 2013918877

ISBN: 978-0615904078

Printed in the United States of America
by CreateSpace, a DBA of On-Demand Publishing, LLC.

*This book is dedicated to Mary,
my unwitting muse.*

Acknowledgements

This book is the product of motivation from numerous sources. Certainly there are people who deserve credit and are not mentioned here. Any such omissions are not intentional and their contributions are appreciated if not explicitly recognized. Cindy Lair and Sue King provided early encouragement about my writing as have various members of AllPoetry.com, including Julia Blacke, Jack Campbell, Allen Bacon, and Jo Hartmann to name a few. Myriad other AllPoetry members have commented on individual poems giving both praise and critique. Also Writing Our Way (WOW), a Great Falls writer's group, provided extensive support and comments. Dr. Marinn Pierce explained the concept of acedia, which resulted in both a poem and the title of this collection. Kristen Perry gave the gentle shove to get serious and publish. Marge Hulburt provided a greatly appreciated editorial review of the final draft, and Jill Kanewischer examined the proof copy when I had simply become too close to it A special note of gratitude to Mary Christiaens, the one who awakened the poet within.

Contents

A Four-sided Triangle	1
Neverwas	2
Loss	3
G. E. M.	4
Just Desserts	6
Love's Call	7
I Don't	8
Acedia	9
Quantum Life	10
My Icon	11
Grace	12
Who is God?	13
Mobius	14
Counsel Keep	15
Betrayed	16
To *My* Immortal Beloved	17
Lost	18
Snow	20
Sacrifice	20
Company	21
One Winter Night	22
RavenTotem	23
The Good Man	24
A Slip of Reality	25
What's In A Name?	26
A Thought	27
Keep Writing	28
Two Feet	29
A Rough Diamond	29
Lost In Space	30
Déjà Vu (All Over Again)	31
The Truth?	32
Hopeless	32

Contents (cont.)

She Is Not Dead 33
Why 34
Job Fails 35
Demons In The Dark 36
Nevermore 37
Three Little Words 38
The Fun House Mirror 40
Shoulds & Oughts 41
Patience 42
Mobius 2.0 42
Heart-string Four Hands 43
Mythos 44
Haunted 46
I Don't (V 2.0) 47
Purgatory 48
The Desperation of a Silent Voice 49
Elemental Women 50
Just Five Feet 51
Karma 52
Am Ende 53
A Cornelian Dilemma 54
Pain 55
Meditation 56
Flame 57
Healing? 58
My Heart's Desire 60
Adoration 61
Into The Box...Again 62
Affirmation 63
Hope Is Gone 63
With Apologies to Robert Service 64
Longing 65
The Pearl 66

Contents (fin.)

One of Life's Little Mysteries	67
Reduced to Writing Poems on a Napkin in a Bar	68
Love	69
M. Emcee	70
Refuting Einstein	70
Sitting	71
Affliction	72
Puzzle Sonnet	73
A Mustard Seed	74
An Harmonic Convergence of Despair	75
Kismet	76
Another Desert Solitaire	77
Happy Valentine's	78
Reduced to Writing Poems on a Napkin in a Bar II	79
The Path	80
Bifurcated	80
Swept Away	81
Decline	82
Passion	83
Hero's Journey	84

An act of love that fails is just as much a part of the divine life as an act of love that succeeds, for love is measured by its own fullness, not by its reception.
— Harold Loukes

A Four-sided Triangle

Love is desire.
Love is attraction.
Love is a touch.
It is compassion.

The Mind is controlling. The Mind is memories. The Mind is distant. It is regret.	The Body is beauty. The Body is angry. The Body is grace. It is afraid.
The Spirit is strong. The Spirit is gentle. The Spirit is brave. It is uncertain.	And, I am lonely. I am hopeful. I am in pain. I am alive.

Neverwas

"I'm miserable," you said to me,
    "And lonely,"
While I wondered how to reach you.

"Yes," was all you said to me
    And shrank,
When I tried to comfort you.

"I have things too," you said to me
    And tapped,
While I stood there amazed.

"For my old age," you said to me
    And looked,
When we talk of her growth.

"It would be nice," you said to me,
    "And fun,"
When I asked if I could help.

"I like you too," you said to me
    And blushed,
While my confusion grew.

"It feels safe," you said to me,
    "And strong,"
While my arms wrapped around you.

"You're kind of cute," you said to me
    And beamed,
While my heart soared.

"I don't think so," you said to me
      And smiled,
When I last asked for a walk.

"Not very good," you said to me
      And fumed,
When I told you what I'd done.

"There is no hope," you said to me
      And glared,
While I stood there devastated.

"We can't be friends," you said to me
      And bristled,
While I froze and died inside.

Loss

Hollow
        vacant
              void.
Empty
      poured-out
                cup.
Withered
        dried-up
              husk.

     My soul.

G. E. M.

I have green-eyed pet within,
    A small and scaly denizen.
It lives inside my heart and mind.
    Its presence there is not benign.

The little thing seldom appeared,
    But when its ugly head it reared,
It did come forth with awesome power
    And strove to linger hour by hour.

Occurrences were rare and brief,
    But I blown about like a leaf
Was caught in such a fearsome grip
    My mind from me it seemed to strip.

I could not reason, could not think,
    Could only under its spell sink.
I moved about trapped in its power.
    My very being it did devour.

It surfaced less with passing years,
    And thus did pacify my fears.
So brief the tenure of its reign,
    I thought its power began to wane.

Until one day it came to pass,
    I chanced upon a charming lass.
She has a friend by name of Steve,
    And he would cause my soul to grieve.

I'd see them here, I'd see them there,
    I'd bump into them everywhere.
With every random happenstance,
    My impish fiend would start to dance.

This little beast would find it meet
    To grab my brain and seize my feet
To take me where I would not go
    And thus to cause me awful woe.

Exigency was fierce and strong.
    For her companionship I'd long.
So then I did such foolish things
    And ripped apart my own heart strings.

A valiant prince did try to warn
    Me of the hurt that could be born
From this creature uncontrolléd
    Such message missed as I thus read.

I loathe this thing, I hate it so,
    With all my will wish it to go,
And I cannot yet to divine
    The means to drive it from my mind.

My jealousy has cost me dear
    And played in to my greatest fear.
With Steve she now doth seek to be
    And will have naught to do with me.

Yet hope, like some small furled leaf,
    Doth push up through this mire of grief,
Perchance the circumstance to mend
    And thus regain my long-lost friend.

Just Desserts

She's not the love that you deserve
    My mother said to me,
But I was bound by fear and guilt
    And would not break away.
A score-and-half of years flew by
    And with them distance grew.
Thus did I find myself estranged
    From wife and all we knew.

Fate took the reins and drove me to
    A place so new and strange.
Where I met one who catalyzed
    A ramifying change.
Yet time was just not right for her;
    It was not opportune.
So over months of trial and pain
    I found myself alone.

Another form has come to me
    And entered in my sphere.
And there again that old refrain
    Is ringing in my ear.
She's not the one that you deserve,
    A friend unto me said
But still I find I think of her:
    She's stuck inside my head.

The one I want is far and gone,
    And she is here and now.
She may be less than I deserve:
    That matters not somehow.
The die is cast, the course is set,
    The race shall soon be run.
So she will soothe my soul for now
    Until I find the one.

Love's Call

Love calls us to seek and embrace
    The things within we cannot face.
She says it's for the best, you know
    Because it helps us heal and grow.

Love calls us to be hale and strong
    In seeking for the things we long,
And when we find ourselves too weak
    To turn to Him for comfort seek.

Love calls us to be meek and kind
    Even when we're disinclined
To treat each other with such care.
    It calls us not unto despair.

The call of Love is often found
    Where human strength has run aground.

I Don't

You said he doesn't get it when
  You tell him there's no hope
For anything between you two.

    In fact, you're right: I don't.

How can you stand so close to me
  To share a common space?
How can you let me hold you in
  A warm and tight embrace?

How can you take another hug
  When of myself I give?
How can you take these things away
  And expect me to live?

How can the message be so clear
  That issues from your lips?
Just to be confounded by
  Your body's little slips.

You said he doesn't get it in
  The February chill.
And once again you are so right:

    Perhaps I never will.

Acedia

There is a space, a hollow void
    That most do choose to shun.
Within the breast, nearby the heart
    Where lie the deeds we've done.

There we must fly a hurt to heal
    Regardless of the source
And so reside enduring pain
    'Til it has run its course.

After a time most choose to flee,
    And dare not to remain,
For therein lies despondency
    Of endless drear refrain.

Out of it flows such mammoth fear
    And doubt laced with regret.
To stare down painful memories
    We'd just as soon forget.

For all our blunders, foibles, gaffs
    Are slowly brought to light
Yet without any means at all
    To put the slightest right.

This place it has a pretty name
    That is not fierce or fell
Acedia is what it's called;
    Another word for Hell.

Quantum Life

All Hallow's Eve: The veil is thin
    Or that is what they say.
The boundary 'twixt life and death
    Does easily give way.

Yet other borders too are filled with
    Holes and perforations.
For those who see the other side 'tis
    Cause for lamentations.

Therein to view what might have been;
    A prospect so foretold.
To see a shade of phantom life
    As thus it might unfold.

To glimpse a spectral happiness
    There lying out of grasp.
To long and plead and bargain 'til
    One breathes their final gasp.

To know desire that won't be filled;
    A never-ending thirst.
To want the best, what might have been,
    And only know the worst.

To watch a while that other self
    Who lives their life complete.
And wonder at a means to change
    The placement of one's feet.

Ah, there must be some magic way.
    Our lives to be exchanged.
For me to know such joyful bliss
    And them to bear such pain.

But until then one's lot is set,
    And as the Path doth wend,
Hope's ghost does make to carry on;
    To play out to the end.

My Icon

That bond
Still draws me back
Where I would not go.
Try as I might
There is no one but you.

Grace

So weary of this track I grow
    With all that I have come to know
About myself that I must face
    And find no hope but saving grace.

So many on me do rely
    See something there within my eye
That helps them still to carry on
    Although my faith is all but gone.

Yet there is One to sit and wait
    For me now to repudiate
Those many things where I find fault
    And bring self-loathing to a halt.

To find in me the inner man
    Who knows he does the best he can
And for some lack within the soul
    To lean on Him to make it whole.

Thus with the journey so begun
    I find no other course to run
For should I yield to all the pain
    I fear my quest will be in vain.

I'll not go back to who I was.
    The knowledge gained will be the cause
To keep me in this Hellish place
    Or force me on to run the race.

For I can see Her by my side
    Who matches me long stride for stride,
And should I falter at the pace
    Will bear me on with healing grace.

Who is God?

Who is this God? To where has He flown
    Leaving a void on this huge golden throne?
I AM STILL HERE, AND I SHALL NOT DEPART.
    I SIT ON THE THRONE THAT ABIDES IN YOUR HEART.

Who is this God? Why is She not near,
    Abandoning me to my doubt and fear?
I AM NEARBY, AND I WILL HOLD YOU CLOSE
    OH, YOU WHOM I LOVE AND DO CARE FOR THE MOST.

Who is this God? When will It release
    The love and the joy that I desperately seek?
THOSE THINGS ARE IN YOU, I THINK YOU WILL FIND,
    AND NEED JUST A HINT OF THAT FACT TO REMIND.

Who is this God that does love me so
    When even myself cannot kindness show?
I AM THE ONE WHO SEES YOU AT YOUR BEST;
    GIVING MYSELF HAVE ERASED ALL THE REST.

Mobius

Get out of bed.
Shave, shower and dress.
Off to work
And make a buck.
Come home to
Tend the house,
Then off to bed.
Repeat *ad infinitum*.

Where is the value
Of such a life?
Where is the purpose
And/or the joy?
Do others find
This treadmill fulfilling?
Where is the companion
To give it all meaning?

Counsel Keep

I, Theoden, sit enthralled
    By one who speaks to seal my doom.
Who lives within my castle walled
    With words to make this place a tomb.

Oh, Wormtongue whispers in my ears
    Thoughts aimed to magnify his power
Through playing on my greatest fears
    My independence to devour.

He sees me weakly, sees me flawed
    And fit to bend unto his will.
I harken as the voice of God
    Thus aid his mission to fulfill.

I need some hero, mage, or guide
    Informéd of the proper view.
I seek the place he does reside
    Just waiting there life to renew.

The battle will be pitched and fierce
    For Wormtongue's stranglehold to break,
But I shall win though gravely pierced
    For it is but my soul at stake.

Alone I'll not this quest complete;
    By aid of champion be set free.
Yet through great irony 'tis meet
    The savior that I seek is me.

Betrayed

Somehow life has allowed me drop
    Into a never-ending well.
To only plummet and ne'er stop
    Along this journey dark and fell.

Was this the overarching plan;
    A destiny of careworn life?
An outline for the son of man
    Thus facing toil and pain and strife?

Or did I somehow fabricate
    The road on which my feet do trod
As if so to retaliate
    For sins against both man and God?

The answer here it matters not,
    For this is where myself I find
And so must carry out my lot
    Of the most sad and loathsome kind.

To *My* Immortal Beloved

I love you.

It doesn't matter
Whether you are
With me or not.
I love you.

It makes no difference
If you return
My affection.
I love you.

It is irrelevant
If you are in love
With someone else.
I love you.

It is of no consequence
Even if you
Despise me.
I love you.

Unless I choose otherwise,
Nothing can alter
This simple fact:
I love you.

Lost

I surveyed mountain vistas vast
    Thought to myself, *I'm home at last.*
For I believed that I had found
    A place where my life could abound.

Yet little did I realize
    The scope of cruel Fates' next surprise.
On such a journey dark and fell
    They've found it meet me to propel.

To drive me far away from peace
    (On bended knees I've sought release)
And to some hell-bound nether space
    Where shreds of ravaged life I face.

Now of my losses take account,
    An open vein where blood does fount,
And as my life begins to fade
    I see my faults so oft replayed.

I hurt a friend, someone held dear,
    No chance to make amends I fear.
I strove and fought to put her past
    Something I have achieved at last,
And now I find to my dismay
    I have completely lost my way.

Trapped in a life of meaning void,
    Someone with whom the gods have toyed,
I had ambitions, plans, and schemes,
    Which all have come to naught, it seems.
So now I seek to find a way
    To carry on from day to day.

Thus, as confusion mounts and grows
    It builds the list of dreadful woes
I do things that I'd rather not
    Because they are with such risk fraught.
And yet they seem to soothe and calm,
    Provide a veil of healing balm.

I fear, in truth, they just conceal
    The horrid wound that will not heal.
Life has become a tangled mess
    That holds no joy, I must confess.

Yet thus my friends do so observe
    And thereon mark that I deserve
Great compliments and lauded praise,
    Such actions do me still amaze.

But as I seek and strive and try
    My malady to pacify
Those thoughts come always to this is end:
    I must make peace with my lost friend.

Snow

Frozen...
        like stars out in space.

Silent...
        as between heartbeats.

Whiteness...
        drifting down slowly.

Crystals...
        such dreams given form.

Sacrifice

If I truly loved her
I would let her go.
Break all the links
I forged between us,
Eliminate any desire to
Ever see her again.
I am not certain
I can love her that well.

Company

I chanced to meet a kindred soul.
    A girl who bore the pain I know.
For she, it seems, had lost someone
    And had her healing trek begun.

We so did forge a common bond.
    Of one another became fond,
And oft the night did while away
    With all the things we had to say.

Yet now she has a new love found,
    Which undermines our common ground
Because she is so bright and gay
    While I still feel I've gone astray.

So though we good friends do remain
    Despite an undercurrent strain;
That love-struck look within her eye
    Does serve my loss to magnify.

One Winter Night

The silence fills the void.
    The blackness is complete.
There is no sound at all
    Save the muttering of the geese.

A soul figure walks alone.
    The cold his brutal cloak.
Snow, it lines the asphalt path
    Where he had trod before.

The mighty Mo' does follow along
    And lit by blue-bulbed light
As to create surreal tableau.
    The stage has been well set.

He sees a bench,
    A stayed landmark
And from him now erupts
    A single cry, despairing fraught.

"You broke my heart,
    (*name withheld here*)!"
So panic all the geese,
    And thus the World moves on.

Raven Totem

An inky bird as black as night,
    The bearer of the sacred light,
Does play about in winds on high
    A silhouette against the sky.
At once a sage and fool he be
    A feather-cloaked dichotomy.
This jester and a joker wild
    Does seek to help each mother's child
To find their deepest self within
    And so uncover what has been
Concealed by all the scars of pain
    The things we hide and would not feign
To bring into the light of day
    And thus to let them fade away.
This wingéd Puck will not let rest
    Those things now burdened in our breast.
And so it is with dharma fraught,
    He carries out his sacred lot
To bring about such change in men
    That they might truly live again
And so to grow in boundless love
    For all down here and those above.

The Good Man

"Oh, you are such a good man, sir."
    They laud him with great praise,
Not discerning all the torments
    And trials he must face.

"Oh, you are such a kind man, sir."
    His adulators sing,
Not knowing how just hard it is
    To do the proper thing.

"Oh, you are such a deep man, sir."
    They find him to be wise,
Not seeing novice, 'prentice, fool
    All lurking there inside.

A deep and kind and goodly soul,
    That is the World's clear view,
Yet down inside his heart he knows
    Acclaim has gone askew.

A Slip of Reality

  A slip of reality.
         Which way does
     The river flow?
            Time, a
   defective
        Watch, runs first
     Fast then slow.

         The cheat of perception,
  A touchstone of truth,
     Without base in substance.
  A collection of knowledge
     Should lead to wisdom;
  Just facts in abundance.

       Nothing is real
   And reality nothing
Save the touch of a hand.

What's In A Name?

What's in a name?
That which we call a rose
Would ne'er prick as hard
Nor hurt so much
Without that sweet-soft name.

What's in a name?
A mystic force that serves
To rack the soul
And wring the heart
Whene'er it is invoked.

What's in a name?
A near misstep of
A moniker nigh bestowed
That's followed me through my life;
A debted beggar owed.

So why is it then
Be these just names
That they seem a web to weave
And with each loop of alpha-silk
Do seek my doom to seal?

A Thought

I think I overthink...I think.
    And complicate the world.
To try and understand too deep
    Just what is at me hurled.

'Tis better far to let things come
    As down life's stream they flow
Than there to sift and analyze
    For what I ought to know.

Yet as I sit and think this thought
    And do on it reflect
It really doesn't fit me well:
    The thing is now suspect.

I thought I overthought...I think
    But now am not so sure.
Perhaps it's simply who I am,
    And what I must endure.

Keep Writing

So sit and think and ponder still
    With fingers wrapped about a quill
Whence on this road of care so paved
    Did one become bound and enslaved.

As words flow from the slender tip
    That daren't escape a fellow's lip
A place that's safe from hazard fraught
    For laying out each madman's thought.

Across the parchment drags the pen
    Like feet in an unending fen
Exploring each nook and crevasse
    Seeking a vaulted truth at last.

And thus the words accumulate
    An effort to illuminate
Those mysteries deep and profound
    Yet only questions do abound.

Two Feet

One solidly fixed unto the ground.
The other planted firmly in mid-air.
Living a life of mundane duties.
Knowing what cannot be seen.
Work a job, pay the bills.
Aware of far too many things.
One by years of training forged.
The other thrust upon me hard.
They pull and tug, these disparate feet,
Slowly rending me asunder.

A Rough Diamond

I
Do
Find
That now
I am losing most
Of my desire to persevere longer
Thus soon I will
Fail and
Quit
It
!

Lost In Space

My thoughts;
Hydrogen molecules bouncing
Throughout the Universe
Spinning
Colliding
Each encounter inducing
A new random direction
Free
Careless
Abstract...

Until they are captured
By the black hole of
Remembering you

To be
Crushed

To a
Singularity

Of despair.

Déjà Vu (All Over Again)

Here he comes again, and with him
that selfsame sick sinking feeling.
It's been six months since the last time;
Was the day before Thanksgiving--
Not much to be thankful about.

Who is he? Well, that much I know.
And why are we still connected?
I don't care for him; a feeling
that is decidedly mutual.
If I never see him again...

She is our only common bond.
We kept stumbling over each
other when I could still see her,
and we continue to do so
even though I may no longer.

Who is he to her? No idea,
And for that soul understanding
I would gladly give up anything.
His visage is another crushing
reminder of whom I have lost.

The Truth?

I feel you everywhere I am.
The more I want to release you,
The more you dominate my mind.
Other women feel vaguely familiar,
And yet it is you that I desire.
The connectedness is real and mysterious;
Tangible and inexplicable.
I am so weary, so tired, so ready to move on:
Those last five words; a simple lie.

Hopeless

I need a balm unto my soul,
A release from my pain
And confusion.
Good comes from suffering;
That trite cliché,
Something I am ready to receive.
Is there no meaning, no reason,
No hope to be found?
Of course not; only giving
Without end until the end.

She Is Not Dead

She is not dead: She lives and breathes.
    She has no mortal hurt endured.
Her face is plain for all to see,
    And now a long life seems assured.

She walks about this Big Sky land
    And leaves her footprints on this place.
As those who see her stop and stand
    Exuding charm with style and grace.

She goes about and runs her life.
    Challenged still, I do suspect.
Seems heedless of great care and strife;
    A victim of benign neglect.

She is not dead clear as can be
    To anyone except for me.

Why

I am merely three-years old.
"WHY?" they question at this age.
That is all I want to know.

Why did you make me love you so?
Leave passion in my soul to rage.
I am merely three-years old.

Why could you not like love to grow?
My care for you you'd surely gauge.
That is all I want to know.

Why could you not the truth me show?
I have no wisdom like some mage.
I am merely three-years old.

Why did you then toward him flow?
Abandon me to vacant stage.
That is all I want to know.

Why does my love for you still glow?
Fifty years soon turns its page.
Yet, I am merely three-years old.
And that is all I want to know.

Job Fails

A curse on ye infernal gods
    For giving me this path to plod
Without hope, succor, or surcease:
    A lonesome journey lacking peace.

Thou hast no need of sparing rods,
    A curse on ye paternal gods,
As thou dost bend me to thy will
    By choking down each bitter pill.

I mark the passing of each day
    And so my life do while away.
A curse on ye eternal gods
    While I do bear life's weary hods.

Thus filled with horror and remorse
    For following this careworn course
My voice this anthem freely lauds;
    A curse on ye internal gods.

Demons In The Dark

They billow forth and siege our sleep,
   Those demons in the dark.
Assailing respite that we seek,
   The demons in the dark.

Let slip as if the Dogs of War
   They plunder through our slumber.
Cry havoc and create furor
   To shred our nights asunder.

When we're alone in waves they come,
   The demons in the dark.
As each one suffers their fate from,
   Those demons in the dark

Our hopes and schemes, such stuff of dreams,
   Our demons in the dark.

Nevermore

"Oh Lord, what fools these mortals be,"
    Observéd Puck whence he did view
Us in the thrall of love and see
    The massive madness forth we spew.

"Oh Lord, what fools these mortals be."
    From Man to ass and back again
Upsetting native harmony
    Each transformation racking pain.

"Oh Lord, what fools these mortals be."
    Thus, penned the Bard to grant reprieve
To each soul of Humanity
    As chased a heart-path ill-conceived.

"Oh Lord, what fools these mortals be."
    Ne'er more these words be spake of me.

Three Little Words

"I love you."

"You can't!
You don't
even know me."

Whereupon,
I proceed
to describe
you to a tee--
justifying
my position?

"I love you."

"No, you don't."

Now who are
you to tell me
who I am
or how I feel?
Are you within
me bearing
the torment of
hopeless longing?

"I love you."

"I know."

So closer to
the truth
we come.
You will
my care
admit
and yet
not admit.

"I love you."

"I wish you didn't."

Now to the rub;
my affection,
it is real
to you and
in your kindness
would spare me
pain of what I
may not share.

"I love you."

The air is still.
No longer may
I speak to you
of how I feel...
or anything.
Yet feeling
still swirls
making life
unbearable.

The Fun House Mirror

Who is it that can see themselves
   With no reflecting wall;
To discern who they really are
   With bumps and warts and all?
And who is it not drawn unto
   That horrid, freakish view?
The one that makes us look our worst
   And wish we could eschew.
The one that gives us a big nose
   Or beady, squinty eyes.
That captures all our tiny flaws
   And of them magnifies.
The one that draws us like a bean
   Or makes us short and wide,
Such glass exposes everything
   That we would seek to hide.
How can we truly see ourselves
   When on that one piece fixed?
Must close our eyes to just move on
   And see what's in the next.

Shoulds & Oughts

I see those fateful letters
Form that tempting, luscious name;
Sitting there, mocking me,
Taunting me to go to a place
I should not, may not go,
For there I risk everything,
Especially my soul.

Why does the Universe
Conspire to place her
Always before my face?
Do I not torment myself
Enough with memories,
Dreams, and longing?
Is tinder to the fire needed?

I have so many
Prospective means
To slake my rapacious need
To reconnect with her,
Yet shun them all
In some ascetic discipline
Of self-crucifixion.

Why do I feel her loss
So acutely, such that all other
Failures pale in comparison?
Do not others of her
Sex find me witty,
Charming and attractive?
Yet none suffice but her.

Patience

How long will I keep myself on tenter's hooks,
How long will I hold this place for you,
How long will my poems pose such questions,
How long until I can know what's true?

Yet I see your action reflected by other souls,
Perceive the distance, the pulling away.
Am I indeed so difficult to bear,
Have so little substance and caché?

Mobius 2.0

Everyone since; just distraction,
Some fleshly goad spurring the action
To purge you from my mind and heart,
And with each failing, falt'ring start
My thoughts to you do bend and sway
Just as those others fade away.

Heart-string Four Hands

A nestled hand does cause my thoughts to flow
    With inklings of bewilderment so mixed.
Therefrom old feelings doth begin to grow;
    Those that cause my soul to be now so vexed.

Present palm settled in mine here and now.
    Does kindle flames of raw and grave remorse.
From a time past by magic linked somehow.
    When I joined another with markéd force.

That hand, a phantom now, I oft recall.
    Wonder at the cause of it, yet known well.
Pressed palm to palm, mine large and her's so small.
    Your warm soft touch and ardor starts to swell.

A mere remembrance of one now gone.
    Your shape, care, and touch for her make me long.

Mythos

Great Chiron was a regal steed
    Atopped by manly bust.
The leader of the centaurs was
    Above desire and lust.

As a healer and a mystic,
    A tutor of renown,
He taught the greatest heroes found
    For many leagues around.

He guided mighty Hercules
    In sword and sling and bow
And as payment for his troubles
    Received protracted woe.

For so his student wounded him,
    While practicing his art,
Shooting his master in the leg
    With Hydra-poisoned dart.

The injury, it would not heal
    For death in it did lie.
Yet poor Chiron was immortal
    And therefore could not die.

So thus it was he did endure
    An unrelenting pain.
A remedy for which he sought
    And strove but all in vain.

Until one day Prometheus
    He found bound to a stone
And said, "Your burden I will take
    To keep as if mine own."

With place exchanged and limbs so bound
    And vulture at his side,
There lingered noble Chiron 'til
    Eventually he died.

Now I am not some epic beast
    Of myth, renown, and fame,
Yet knowledge of unhealing wounds,
    I understand the same.

For I too struggle mightily
    For respite and relief,
From piercéd heart and savaged soul
    Seek balm be it so brief.

So Chiron's tragic saga has
    To me the key revealed;
The means from which this malady
    Might finally be healed.

The only way to save one's soul
    And thus regain their life
Is freely give it all away
    In total sacrifice.

Haunted

It doesn't matter what I do
I fail to move on.
Distractions serve to salve my soul
But do not solve a thing.

To fight and strive and struggle hard
To put you in the past
All seem to come to no avail
I am still drawn to you.

This makes no sense! I haven't seen
You now for months on end.
Short span of days creates a space
Where we may meet again.

Will he be there, will you see me
And how will you react?
Such thoughts do plague my mind
To mystical effect.

There are folk that ease the ache
That lurks within my heart.
But in the dead, still, calm of night
'Tis you that haunts my peace.

The more I try to draw away and
Find a life apart.
The more the pull and tug I feel
That strains upon my heart.

I Don't (V 2.0)

I don't hug women I hardly know,
    Hold them close crying out their soul,
Except for you.

I don't contrive to share a kiss,
    And sear the heart with rampant bliss,
Except with you.

I am not forward. I do not press.
    Undo a button. Caress a breast.
Except with you.

I don't hold children on my lap,
    And keep them from their nightly nap,
Except with you.

I don't go crazy or misbehave,
    Lose my mind to rant and rave,
Except for you.

I don't wake up and pine away,
    Losing sleep 'til break of day,
Except for you.

Purgatory

So here I sit and do languish.
    Just to escape my single wish
From situation, act, and deed.
    My soul desire but to be freed.

I feel you come, do know you're near,
    Which simply fills my heart with fear
Of how and when and where we'll meet,
    And thus my visage you will greet.

Once there I stood at head of stair
    To see you sit and not to dare
Approach the door thus held by me
    And so begin to set me free.

Then as I watched you shun my form
    Within me rose a grief forlorn
With memory of another day
    When you were glad I came your way.

I gazed at you just long enough
    To know you wouldn't call my bluff,
And then with heart so far from gay,
    I simply turned and walked away.

My spine as rigid as a rod,
    So down the asphalt I did trod
Without a backward glance to hint
    How much encounter might have meant.

I cannot find the means too soon
    To bind and heal this karmic wound.
Yet not unless you share my will,
    My mending ways are be born still.

The Desperation of a Silent Voice

You tried to tell me
Without speaking
All the things you felt.
Your eyes conveyed the
Thoughts unwanted,
Wherein your heart they dwelt.
Your actions spoke through
Megaphones the
Things you would not own.
While fervently
I did attend to
Gesture, look, and tone.

Your words denied most
Everything that
Other means proclaimed.
A risk too great
To be exposed and
By such be defamed.
Thus, through my want to
Understand your
Wrath on me did fall.
I sought to have
Your company but
Rather found a wall.

Elemental Women

First of all there's Mary,
    My airy, faerie icon,
Who floated down into my life
    And now has drifted on.
She has wrought such change in me
    My former self I cannot see.

Next follows spritely Danica,
    My charming fire-brand.
The blood it curséd through my veins
    When e're she held my hand.
Barest tug of gossamer thread
    And we'd have fallen into bed.

And then comes stalwart Cindy,
    My firmly grounded one.
She adds such joy to dull, drab life;
    My time with her is fun.
She helps me with my task to toil
    And for ideas is unmatched foil.

Last, not least, there's Laura,
    My long-time watery friend.
Our work while here is boundaries
    That ebb and flow and bend;
Linkages quite complicated
    Of our lives together fated.

These four are fateful come to me
    To balance out my life,
To help me with the challenges,
    Of which my time is rife.
I'm grateful for each one of them
    And pleased to count them as a friend.

Just Five Feet

Why do you mean so much to me:
    Why can't I let you go?
Why do I feel so bound to you
    Like no one else before?

I have a strong need to take care
    Of those whom I hold dear.
It validates my own self worth
    And pacifies my fear.

And yet with you the draw extends
    Beyond all time and space.
Wild feelings stir here in my chest
    When e're I see your face.

I do not want to be this way,
    So locked within your thrall,
But without some means yet unfound
    Cannot escape at all.

Karma

How is it words
Can haunt our lives?
Or some old place
Does thrust us back?

Just hear a phrase,
The memory floods
To sweep away
All reasoned thought.

A sight, a sound
A smell, a touch.
My own voice
did recall my doom.

"I don't want
to talk to you,"
The last words she
Ever spoke to me.

Am Ende

I just want to quit…everything.
I am so tired of feeling empty.
I cannot find the path.
I am lost without the benefit
of not knowing where I am.
I am alone in the masses.
I do not want to be open any more.
I do not want to trust.
I do not want to need.
I want to regain my self-sufficiency…
lost, crushed, and stolen away.
I cannot find solace, only pain.
I cannot have the things that would give me surcease.
I cannot say the words that would set me free.
I cannot see the person who could make me whole.
I cannot have the knowledge that could break my chains.
I am trapped, and I am doomed.
I am desperately tired of being me…
whoever that is.

A Cornelian Dilemma

How does one keep oneself alive
    To face the adversary great?
How does one with a purpose strive
    And struggle against a cruel fate?

How does one keep their spirits high
    When all the world does tug them down?
Why then not offer up a sigh
    And slip beneath the waves to drown?

The answer is to me unclear:
    Why not to cut the mortal bond?
The end of life I do not fear;
    To halt the pain that just goes on.

The greatest thing that stays my hand...
    The hurt to those who with me stand.

Pain

I used to be oh so okay
    To live my life alone.
A solitude that I enjoyed
    As round the world I'd roam.
But you have robbed me of that skill,
    The lost forgotten knack.
So now with each dull passing day
    I sorely feel the lack.

You said you didn't understand
    My doing things solo.
And I replied to you, if not
    I'm unsure I would go.
Yet now I feel the pain acute,
    A loss so magnified,
For it was bliss to walk the world
    With you there by my side.

I didn't need you all the time
    For solace without end.
It was enough to look around
    And know you were my friend.
I seek for one to fill the void
    And so to take your place.
But no soul seems available
    To fill that empty space.

I wasn't looking very hard
    When you I chanced to find.
I fear I'll not find someone else
    Until you flee my mind.

Meditation

Breathe in.
Imagine you're walking.
Hear the birds, see the sky, feel the grass.
No! Walking reminds me of her!
Hearing the birds, watching the sky,
Walking, talking, bonding.
Breathe out.

Breathe in.
While walking you see a house
A most inviting, welcoming house.
No, not her house!
The one where I felt warm, safe, and loved.
The house to which I may never return.
Breathe out.

Breathe in.
You walk up the steps.
Open the door to the inviting house.
No, not her steps!
The ones where I stood as I knocked on her door
and waited for her sunny, enchanting smile.
Breathe out.

Breathe in.
You enter the house and
walk into a close, cozy kitchen.
No, not her kitchen!
The one where we lingered and talked.
Where she drew up near to hold me close.
Breathe out.

Breathe in.
In the kitchen you see a table
with dishes, and silverware.
No, not her table!
The one covered with the trappings of her life.
A reminder of how I loved her...still love her.
Breathe out.

Breathe in.
On the table you see a lemon.
Cut a slice and bite it.
Sour! The shock breaks the spell.
I am free from her again...
for this moment, at least.
Breathe out.

Flame

I light this candle
In honor of you,
In regard for all
That you have done for me.

I watch this candle
In memory of you,
To remind me of the
Merging of two souls in need.

I put out this candle
In affection for you,
To release the love
I still feel into the Universe...

That it may find you.

Healing?

We try to fix my mind, you see,
   With different sorts of chemistry.
The problem is I greatly fear
   My difficulty isn't there.

The challenge that I must now face
   Is to seek out that hidden place.
To find the source of all this pain;
   A quest thus far I make in vain.

It seems a hole within my chest
   Describes the malady the best,
Which makes me wonder if my heart
   Is not the proper place to start.

Yet medicine, that science fine,
   Cannot a method to divine
The means to treat a heart that's broken;
   Their efforts there are but a token.

Therapy's another source
   To provide a treatment course,
And while this comes much closer yet
   It still evades a need unmet.

So 'round the problem we all dance
    As fate evolves from happenstance,
And thus avoid the hidden key
    That from this hurt would set me free.

I know what I must needs to do,
    A task I heartily eschew.
I cannot bear the risk to take,
    My hopes all on one moment stake.

For she who holds the answer close,
    The one for whom I care the most,
Lives safe behind a fortress wall
    And will not deal with me at all.

Yet someday I'll approach that gate
    To sit there patiently and wait
For her therein to me reveal
    Those things perchance my soul to heal.

So until then I try to cope
    With phantom life and faded hope.
Forbearing 'til my Mary dear
    Illuminate this gloom so drear.

My Heart's Desire

Since unto thee I may not speak
   I'll need to find another way
To share the secrets I would leak,
   And thus to tell you all I'd say.

My love for you does still hold strong,
   My care for you is just as great.
To be with you my heart does long.
   'Tis bound to you by strings of fate.

Yet my desire is not confined
   Unto your lithe and curvéd form.
I also seek to share the mind
   And soul your body does adorn.

Moreover, then my thoughts do stray
   Unto someone for whom you care.
I think about her night and day
   And offer up a soulful prayer.

So unto you it might seem strange
   To hold you in such high esteem.
Like from my mind I am deranged
   Or trapped in some nightmarish dream.

Yet I have not my senses left
   Despite the magnitude of pain
As from your company bereft
   I struggle to my life regain.

If I could just one message send,
   I wish for you great happiness.
Repeated now until the end
   Gladly forsaking all the rest.

Adoration

A pedestal's a tricky place
    To put someone you love.
They just may grow accustom to
    The view from up above.
And then again they just might fear
    That they will take a spill.
When of the idol worshiping you
    Find you've had your fill.

An icon is a risky thing
    For one whom you adore.
For they may up and leave you
    Brokenhearted evermore.
It's better all the way around
    To see them as they be,
Thus the burden of perfection
    To always set them free.

These lessons were too lately learned
    I find that I now fear,
And I think that have they cost me
    Someone very near and dear.
But with some luck and fortune fine
    I think that I may see
Another one whom I can love
    And share my time with me.

Into The Box...Again

I am a fearsome shadow who
    But stalks across the land,
Yet as the people watch me pass,
    They see aught but a man.

For though I still do walk about,
    Inside I am but dead.
And so I go about the town
    My heart brim full of dread.

And should I chance upon someone,
    A friend that I might know,
We'll chat a bit, so speaking naught
    Of heart-felt grief and woe.

I mention only niceties
    And from them keep the rest.
So then I sit alone at night
    With horrors in my breast.

I have so few to talk to, or
    With whom my tales I share,
And such is my intensity,
    I think that them I scare.

And there is one with whom I'd speak,
    My stories I would tell,
But any work to meet with her,
    Would send me straight to Hell.

So thus, I cram inside of me
    The words I need to say.
And while they rot away my soul,
    I die some more each day.

Affirmation

Most beautiful of women that
    I have ever seen,
My life is drawn unto you as
    If a waking dream.
Adoration, love, and joy are
    What I felt the most,
And the pain of losing you does
    Haunt me as a ghost.
Roses in my garden scented
    Just like your perfume,
Remind me of a bygone day
    Sitting 'neath the moon.
Yesterday has come and gone to
    Fade into the past,
Yet the memory of you will
    Linger 'til the last.

Hope Is Gone

Hope went into a coma on Father's Day.
    ("Oh, and have a nice one," by the way.)
Hope had a few bouts of consciousness.
    ("How are you doing?" as I sat and gaped.)
Hope died on October 6th of that year.
    ("I don't want to talk to you." *Click*)
Hope might have been heard scratching at the coffin lid.
    (Next time she sees me she'll be happy it happened.)
Hope was exhumed and cremated on November 17th.
    ("Do not approach her, her family, her friends.")
I wish Remembrance would join Hope.

With Apologies to Robert Service

What does one do when they've lost themselves
    And they don't know who they are,
When the craving for just one kindly word
    Will draw them near and far,
When the lightest touch of a fair, soft hand
    Kindles feeling unbidden,
And sends the mind on a worldly race
    Pursuing desires hidden?

What does one do when a single form
    Will stay a longing fierce,
When the thought of her does slay the soul
    And heart with arrows pierce,
When there's no one else to take that place
    And to fill the aching void,
And hope is crushed, then set aflame,
    Thus utterly destroyed?

What does one do when the pain won't end
    And there is no succor nigh,
When memories haunt like sallow ghosts
    That won't lay down and die,
When the present's dead, and the future's gone,
    And the past's far too alive,
And it takes a will of iron and steel
    To just try to survive?

What does one do when they're all bound up
    And locked dire straits,
When looking up and all around
    Just see Hell's blazing gates,
When they contemplate the prospects bleak
    And realize they're doomed?
Why no more than to slip away
    And simply be entombed.

Longing

I sit here now and do reflect
    Upon the pain that lay in store
As I did then draw close to you
    And know the joy that came before.

Of you I wanted many things.
    Desire within my heart still sings.
In grandest dreams a life we'd share
    Filled up with love and hope and care.

Or failing that fast friends we'd be
    And revel in good company.
Our lives would merge and flow and blend
    From now until our time would end.

But tempest Fate had other plans,
    And I played fool into its hands.
I failed to see the threat I bore,
    As I approached Heart's shuttered door.

The loss is simple agony
    Now that you have withdrawn from me
Fueled by the haunting memory
    Of a time you cared for me.

There is no means to hold the past
    To make those vaulted feelings last,
Yet I would seek still to repair
    One another's hurt that's there.

Thus here I sit and more reflect
    Upon the pain that I now bear.
For I did dare draw close to you
    And taste the joy of love so fair.

The Pearl

What would I give for what
    I feel to be untrue?
What would I pay for what
    I see to be a lie?
What would I sacrifice
    To free my soul from you?
What would I do for these
    Dear thoughts from me to hie?

No thing too great to lose
    So that the feelings end.
No price too large for
    Deception full and replete.
No pain too much if
    But it will my heart to mend.
No task too huge that
    It might now the spell complete.

Desire for you, it does
    Consume me utterly.
My need for you extends
    Beyond a mortal bound.
In such a state, I am
    Just a mere shard of me.
Without you, I am lost
    And never to be found.

One of Life's Little Mysteries

Connection 'twixt two.
Bond obscure yet felt.
Such by one denied,
And other embraced.
Vehemently real.

Linkage thus composed.
Chance random meeting.
Similarities
Inexplicable;
Serendipities.

Hallmark of like fate.
Coincidence swells.
Events assuming
Manipulation.
Daimon near at hand.

Cold, rigid die cast.
Vision resolute.
Bright lit path eschewed.
Tight-closed eyes evade.
No escape of hope.

Reduced to Writing Poems on a Napkin in a Bar

I live inside a prison cell
    That no one else can see,
With walls of stone and bars of iron
    And door with hidden key.
Confinement comes from my own mind,
    And it is couched in fear
Of bringing hurt and causing grief
    To one whom I hold dear.

The wicked irony is that
    She no more cares for me,
And greater shame she does not know
    That she could set me free.
I think she fears that my force comes
    From romance that I crave.
That time is past, and now I seek
    My humble soul to save.

Naught but the merest kindly word
    Of her forgiveness spoke
Would serve at once to lose my chains
    And thus release my yoke.
But there is just no hope for me
    Because I may not speak
Unto her of the power she holds
    And how the spell to break.

And so it is I languish here
    As day does pass to day,
And try to face an endless pain
    That will not go away.
I have no hope, I stand no chance
    To ever find release.
This burden I must carry forth
    Until my time does cease.

So now I wait impatiently for
    Me to meet my end,
And as our spirits be reborn
    That we can try again.

Love

Longing over vast expanse
Lingering on void emotions
Lasting out virtual eternity
Likening of vacant enchantment

M. Emcee

You are the inspiration
Of my Dark Night.
You are the muse
That drives my hand.
You who have led me
To the brink of the abyss,
Bowing my stiff neck,
Forcing eyes to gaze inward.

You who have wrought
In me pain and confusion.
You who have roused
My spirit and soul.
You are the source
Of mysteries boundless,
Braiding a path through
Sand, mire, and fog.

Refuting Einstein

Time;
When I was with you,
It had no meaning.

Sitting

Nothing in the span of time,
Nor throughout the march of years
Will take away the memory of
Time that you did spend with me.

Sitting on a large tan rock
Fingers kneading your taut back.
Arms then wrap round your lithesome
Frame easing you into my chest.

Or seated on your well-worn couch
A notion I embraced and moved
Into a space of portent full.
You fell to me my lips to kiss.

Or sitting close-knit, side-by-side
Watching winsome imagery pass
And chatting of the art on-screen
Remembering how it made us feel.

Or seated on your old park bench
Following the children's play
Wrapped in blanket gently close
My hand stroked your long brown hair.

Oh, fire of passion mixed with pain
How bitter-sweet 'tis to recall
All the time you spent with me
And how my love for you it grew.

Affliction

There is a monstrous demon,
    They call the thing a muse,
That makes me defy anyone
    To walk inside my shoes.

The tiny imp has favored games
    Of which it likes to play
To fill my mind with rhyme and verse
    That will not go away.

I wake up 'ere the light of dawn
    With words that must be writ
And chase about for pen and pad
    'Til down with them it sit.

The words they leap from head to page
    As out of me they come
To fill a sheet in hasty scrawl:
    My vomitorium.

But unlike normal purgatives
    Relief is not soon brought.
The poetry that I have spawned
    Consumes my waking thought.

The writings do completely fail
    To soothe my memory
And simply serve to reinforce
    The feelings I would flee.

But maybe it is the process,
    A path that I must trod
That leads me to discovery
    Of man, and self, and God.

And so with weary leaden limbs
    I grab my own lapel.
Then mustering some inner strength,
    I drag myself through Hell.

Puzzle Sonnet

Into a serpent's den you peered and went,
More fearful than at first you might have seemed,
intent on hiding certain thoughts unspent,
sequestered safe within a lucid dream.
secure then ensconced in assured repose,
You carried on throughout the evening bright
of conversation heedless, when arose
unbidden feelings such as came to light.
Desire deep out of your eyes did fall,
and mingled with a more confuséd pain,
no easy path of quick and sure withdrawal
in hopes from wanton impulse to refrain.
carefullest tread did thus your skill enhance
and spared you from a lost, fateful romance.

A Mustard Seed

A quest began within a Source divine.
    Oh, to believe that promise could hold true.
Then off for purpose and fresh meaning find.
    Might see oneself from this vantage anew.

Rest in hope that Fate has not forsak'n all.
    Thus, strive to grow and prosper in one's life.
Put down the fear that such harm shall befall.
    Trust that One certain future outshines strife.

Hallowed plan woven amongst a twisted path.
    Secure harbour hidden in blackest night.
Conduséd course with turns and drifts which hath
    So near eclipsed the Host of faith and light.

Challenged then to go with Grace as we ought,
    Lest that secret plan fail and come to naught.

An Harmonic Convergence of Despair

Longing crushed
      'Twixt mortar of a frozen soul
            And pestle of a stone heart.

Hope dashed
      Upon jagged rocks of regret;
            No lighthouse beacon there.

Love asleep
      Lain out on icy wasteland of isolation;
            A frigid corpse remains.

Friendship abandoned;
      Long dead fingers of a wasted life
            Outstretched to a small warming fire.

Pain abundant,
      No prospect of succor,
            Hurting body and soul without end.

Kismet

Why does it seem to be so hard
    To meet a simple human need?
I merely want someone with whom
    To share my hidden hopes and dreams.

The fairer sex whom I befriend
    Can draw out of me all the best
But never meet that aching need
    That stirs within my hollow breast.

Then nigh to one I'll draw too close
    With whom I feel attraction strong
And drive them far away from me:
    They'll not endure such stress for long.

If there is fault where does it lay?
    My inmost thoughts do give me pause,
Though people like me well enough,
    My mind says that I am the cause.

From many years of marriage drear
    I have emergéd greatly changed.
With thoughts and actions foreign now
    Unto myself I do seem strange.

The craving human company
    Is now a longing far too great
To be dismissed or idly tossed
    To happenstance or random fate.

Now cease to walk this endless road
    That left my feet blooded and torn.
To cast aside all thought of love;
    Immortal burden be still born.

The growth throughout my inner self
    And feelings that do plague me yet
Are nothing save my lot in life;
    The manifest of my kismet.

Another Desert Solitaire

An ocean of sand,
    Such a cliché;
One seldom drowns in such an ocean.

Mountains of sand,
    Grains without number;
Each an opportunity lost or found.

Parched dry sand,
    Void of life's staff;
The matrix of human existence.

Water in sand,
    Brief damp then gone
Except in rare discrete locations.

Life on the sands;
    A few do sink
'Neath granular waves ne'er to rise again.

Love is but sand.

Happy Valentine's

Why can I not just let you go
    And thus allow my heart to grow?
Because hopes so much invested
    Are too much to be bereft of.

Why can I not just let you be
    And thus of pain to be set free?
Because my need for solace great
    Drove me to think I'd found my mate.

Why can I not just let you leave
    And thus allow my soul to grieve?
Because my trust in you did lie
    Too much to watch it fade and die.

Why can I not just let you live
    And thus my love another give?
Because I hold this strong and true
    I'll never find someone like you.

Reduced to Writing Poems on a Napkin in a Bar II

I have two fateful women that
 Within my brain reside.
And for my thoughts they do compete,
 So striving side by side.
Now one has had enough of me
 And so my life has left.
The other finds me bearable
 And I am not bereft
Of her company just yet,
 And still I find I fear
That with the passing of each day
 That portent time draws near.
So now I sit of liquor full
 And mind in such a fog
To write down all my vague concerns
 Upon a napkin log.

The Path

Not a tunnel,
No light at the end,
No road bed to walk on,
No train coming the other way.

It is a mine shaft.
It is a crevasse.
It is an abyss.
It is bottomless.

Unfathomable distance,
Unseen hand afore the face,
Unknown rocks on either side,
Uncertain space and sound and time.

Bifurcated

I don't want to let you go,
And you are already gone.

I don't want to lose you,
And you are already lost.

I don't want to hurt you,
And you are already slain.

I just want to be your friend,
But I am only your enemy.

Swept Away

Emotion it does build in me,
   A fateful draw I wish to flee.
So with the passing of each day
   I fear I might be swept away.

A massive oceanic surge
   Begins my wounded heart to purge,
And ease the soulful pain I felt,
   Which I had though forever dwelt.

'Twas lodged within my ragged breast,
   A searing scar preventing rest.
That succor now I seek to claim,
   As if a moth unto a flame.

I fear to take this road again
   And risk to lose my new found friend.
So many that of late I've lost
   With awful hurt and wretched cost.

Yet betting all I leave the door;
   Might be unshipped and seen no more.
And so as night does change to day
   I feel myself be swept away.

Decline

Slowly away I seem to fade;
    A futile life of masquerade.
Less of myself I seem to be;
    Someone not recognized as me.

The fog around me thickly swirls
    Of memories that flow and furl.
A wise man said it would soon pass,
    Yet it has strove to build and last.

Feelings do make horrendous strain
    Of impulses I must refrain.
To act on them and risk a shattered
    Hope and life all torn and tattered.

Much more of this I cannot bear;
    Sensation flooding everywhere.
I need to rest and cannot find
    A way to drive her from my mind.

Passion

A giant drowsed within my soul.
    'Twas put to rest by years of woe.
Until one day a maiden fair,
    A slender curve with long brown hair,
Did chance upon this beast asleep
    And sitting down began to weep.
Her tears fell on the inert form
    Launching waves of greatest harm.

She roused Colossus from its slumber.
    About my heart it came to lumber.
At first its tread was mild and soft
    As my affections made to loft
Toward this woman sweet and kind.
    I thought up ways to make her mine.

Our time, to start, was full of bliss,
    A heart-felt talk, a tender kiss.
But then the visions became blurred.
    From my attentions she demurred.
The pressures of her other life
    Conspired to wrought within her strife.
Those close to her did shout, "You're mine!"
    A path with me she could not find.

Too late those forces made her flee
    From the monster within me.
Thus looséd from its heart-bound cage
    About my soul it makes to rage.
And now alone I face my foe
    Once put to rest by years of woe.

Hero's Journey

You set out on life's journey
    Full of purpose, full of pride.
You fasten on your armor
    With a sword strapped to your side.

Striding forward, never heeding
    Any prospect of despair,
To meet your fate whatever
    It'll be that 'waits you there.

The years do pass so quickly
    As you move yourself along.
Yet the doubts they creep upon you:
    "Was the path I took far wrong?"

And then some day as Fate is want
    Catastrophe may fall
To break the strut of warrior's march
    Down to an infant's crawl.

The trail that was so brightly lit
    And full of promise seemed
Has turned in to a quicksand
    Sucking down your hopes and dreams.

It is no use to struggle
    Or to rail against the gods.
The best to do is hold on tight
    And simply play the odds.

There's a fair chance that you'll
    Sink down to never rise again.
You'll only know the outcome
    If you push on to the end.

And there is just one surety
    As certain as the grave.
The selfsame path is trodden
    By the coward and the brave.

For it's not the hero's metal
    That's the means to see you through.
It's the will to persevere
    That determines how you'll do.

And you won't come out the other side
    Unchangéd or unmarked.
You will be a different person
    Than the one who did embark.

If you're better for the travel
    Or it simply makes things worse
Is not always apparent
    Though the road you'll surely curse.

You want to reach the finish,
    And you'll bet you're near the end,
But the path seems only endless
    As you round each curve and bend.

As your heart is nigh to breaking,
    And your spirit starts to fail,
"Why hast thou forsaken me?"
    Unto the Sky you wail.

And while I'd like to comfort
    Or to speak some words to help,
I find that I have aught to give:
    I'm on that road myself.

About the Author

Eric worked for over 20 years in a combination of weed and forest science and management across the western US. He has a Master's degree from Colorado State and a Ph.D. from Oregon State. He was a research assistant at both institutions and a professor of Forestry and Natural Resources at the American Samoa Community College.

Rather spontaneously, Eric began writing poetry in late 2008, not having written a single poem in over a decade prior to that. At present, he has composed over 250 poems (which are available at http://allpoetry.com/Terry_F_Ide), with another couple dozen in various stages of development. *Acedia* is Eric's first literary publication.

Eric lives in Great Falls, Montana with his two cats, M.C. Escher and Ginger, and four, "twenty-something" roommates. He works as a cook and handyman to support his affliction of writing.

www.ingramcontent.com/pod-product-compliance
Lightning Source LLC
Chambersburg PA
CBHW032018040426
42448CB00006B/652